The Cruise P

CW00429808

The Fjord People of Norway

By

Sam Hall

©Sam Hall 2018
Published by
www.samhallbooks.com
Dorking, Surrey, UK
ISBN: 9781793165053

The right of Sam Hall to be identified as the
author of this work has been asserted by him in accordance
with the Copyright, Designs and Patents Act, 1988.

ABOUT THE AUTHOR

With nearly 50 years' experience in international journalism and travel, Sam Hall, now retired, worked with all the major news agencies, including Reuters, for whom he was a foreign correspondent for five years and later their Chief Scandinavian correspondent. He was also an on-screen reporter covering the top international stories of the day for ITN's prestigious flagship programme, *News at Ten*.

Travelling to more than 100 countries around the world, he has covered various wars, riots and disturbances including the Nigerian-Biafran civil war, the Turkish invasion of Cyprus, the Siege of Beirut and the Falklands War.

A compulsive traveller, he walked as a young man from Barcelona to Copenhagen and as a middle-aged one nearly 400 miles across the French-Italian Alps in the footsteps of Hannibal, not to mention another 328 miles from his home in Surrey to Lands' End – an epic journey he describes in his book *'Blisters'*.

He is a widely acclaimed enrichment lecturer with 22 years' experience and has travelled the world with all the major cruise lines. He also sailed across the North Sea in an open Viking boat and travelled thousands of miles in the High Arctic. His book *'The Fourth World: The Heritage and Destruction of the Arctic'* is considered a definitive work on the Arctic for which he was likened in his writing to that of Wilfred Thessiger.

Sam is also a film-maker who, in conjunction with the Norwegian TV and film production companies, Bergefilm and Videomaker Nord, has won several international awards. Many of these films have been shown in more than 50 countries worldwide and ultimately earned him a Lifetime Achievement Award by the British company, CS Media.

Sam is also an accomplished lecturer, presenter and conference host, and an acclaimed hyper-realistic artist. You can find more of his books on his website *www.samhallbooks.com*

BOOKS BY SAM HALL

PRONUNCIATION GUIDE

Å/å - as in 'flaw' and 'saw'. i.e. Skageflå=Skah-ge-flaw
Ø/ø - as in 'whirl' 'earstwhile and 'pearl'.
"-vik" is pronounced "veek".
Matvika is pronounced 'Mahtveeka', with a long 'a'.

The Pulpit, Seven Sisters waterfall and Knivsflå farm, Geirangerfjord.

INTRODUCTION

Whenever we talk about the fjords of Norway in any depth, if you will excuse the pun, we should really talk first about the retreat of the last Ice Age when glaciers slid down the mountainsides, breaking off from what then was a massive inland ice cap to create the jords.

Those monumental events have had a major impact on the people of Norway, and particularly on the remarkable people I call "The Real Fjord People" – god-faring farmers and their wives and children, living simple hardworking lives. It was their lot to eke a living as best they could from tiny strips of land at the end of a fjord or beneath the cliffs that rise almost sheer from the waters of the fjords, or from almost inaccessible farms perched on cliff top ledges hundreds of feet above the waterline.

These fjord dwellers had to cope with all kinds of problems caused by the very existence of the fjords. Ever since first learning of their existence I have been inspired by their resilience, toughness, strength of spirit - and above all their extraordinary courage.

This booklet is designed to provide a background to their story and to act as a handy guide to the cliff top and other farms in Geirangerfjord and Sunnylvsfjord, and the events that happened in them.

The best way to use the guide is first to read pages 9-28 before visiting Geiranger, then to read the Sailaway Guide beginning on page 29 as you sail out of the fjord, referring to the map on pages 30-31 and preferably carrying a pair of binoculars. Some of the material in the main section of the booklet is repeated in the Sailaway Guide for your convenience.

I hope that this will give you an insight and a deeper understanding of these very special people and the beautiful fjord in which they lived.

Sam Hall
Chartwood
Dorking
Surrey, UK.

Vesterås Farm, immediately above the jetty
at Geiranger.

LIFE IN THE FJORDS

During the Ice Age about three million years ago, the whole of Scandinavia was covered in ice. Inland, this icecap was a couple of thousand metres thick. The incredible pressure of the surface layers caused ice crystals deep inside the glacier to slide over one another - as if the entire ice cap was moving on a bed of ball bearings. As the pull of gravity dragged the edges of the ice cap downwards, crevasses formed and they became glaciers.

A glacier is like a frozen river. Depending on the conditions, the ice moves anywhere between one foot a day and forty-five feet a day. The steeper the mountainside, of course, the more chaotic the ice fields. The point at which the glacier stops depends largely on climatic conditions. With the effects of global warming, many glaciers in Norway are now three to five miles shorter than they were a few years ago.

As the ice retreated, its massive, grinding weight gouged out the river valleys and left deep basins, which then filled with seawater to become fjords. As because the ice nearer to the coast was thinner and therefore less heavy, the water there is shallower than it is further inland, where the ice was thicker and therefore much heavier.

For this reason, the innermost parts of a fjord are invariably deeper than the sea itself. Thus, the longest fjord in Norway, Sognefjord, which is 204 kilometres or 122 miles long, reaches depths of 1300 metres. That is nearly 4,000 feet, ten times deeper than most of the North Sea.

If you were to place Britain's highest mountain, Ben Nevis, on the bottom of Sognefjord, you would only be able to see the top 44 metres or 130 feet of it above the surface.

That is roughly the height of an average oak tree. Even in these days of satellite photography, no-one really knows exactly how many fjords and inlets there are in Norway because nobody has bothered to count them. We do know, though that the country's entire coastline totals some 1,600 miles or 2,650 kilometres.

If you include the fjords and the peninsulas, the coastline is eight times as long - more than 13,000 miles or 21,000 kilometres, or roughly half the distance around the world!

The fjords of Norway differ greatly. In depth. In length. In breadth. And in character. The chalky green, glacial waters of Fjaerlandsfjord , a northern arm of the great Sognefjord, run 22 miles inland and are just half a mile wide, with the glacier tumbling off the mountains at the top of the fjord.

Trollfjord is even narrower and thus a major tourist attraction. In parts, it is only 100 metres wide , the steel plating of even smaller cruise ships almost scraping the sheer rock walls.

Where there are glaciers and fjords, there are also waterfalls and these play a vital role in the Norwegian economy, tapped for hydro-electric power for industry and local communities. Indeed, the entire country receives its electricity in this way.

Larger fjords, like Sognefjord, are several miles wide and their ecosystems, weather and moods change all the time. And yet, in this wild, often harsh landscape, there are oases of peace - luxuriant and fertile, with flowers and plants you would expect to see only farther south in Europe.

Other, equally wide fjords are centres for water sports, sailing, fishing and small industry. On the banks of these, many villages have grown into towns, some with international reputations. Molde, known as the "City of Roses", for example, is world renowned for its annual jazz festival. Getting to the other side of the fjord, though, is both time-consuming and

expensive. Firstly, you nearly always have to wait for the ferry - and usually

you find you've just missed one.

A ten minute crossing costs 52 Norwegian kroner - that is roughly £4.75 or US $ 6.25 per passenger*. For a car and driver, the cost is dependent on the length of the vehicle. A regular car with driver costs NOK 152 kroner (£13.92/$18.32). A car of 6-7 metres length plus driver would be NOK 368 (£33.75/$52.50) and for a car 7-8 m long NOK434 (£39.75/$52.35). The price scale increased to NOK 1100 (£100.75/$132.60) for vehicles between 19 and 22 metres in length.

So driving a car in Norway can be very expensive. Tunnels are also subject to tolls and drivers also pay to cross the bridges, which are a feature of most main fjords.

In the south, Stavanger is the focal point for Norway's vital offshore oil industry. Once built, the rigs are towed out to sea with extraordinary precision.

One rig comprises an intricate system of wellheads connected to pipelines which snake across the seabed to the base of the rig's concrete support column, which is as high

as the Eiffel Tower is tall. North Sea oil and the offshore industry have had a major impact on Norway's national economy but this has not been achieved without cost.

In March 1980, an accommodation platform attached to

* *Prices as of November 2018*

The Alexander Kjelland rig, sank when one of its giant legs broke off in a gale. One hundred and twenty three men were killed.

Ten centuries of shipbuilding in the fjords has been of enormous benefit to the offshore oil industry. Viking settlements along the fjords communicated - and traded - with one another mostly by sea.

A thousand years ago, the Vikings were building ocean going ships and crossing the North Sea to Britain, Ireland and France, and to Iceland, Greenland and North America when other nations were hugging the coast in little more than coracles and canoes.

The most important trading centre was Norway's second city, Bergen, which calls itself the "Capital of the Fjords" or the gateway to them. By the 13th century, the warren of gabled, wooden buildings that was the hub not only of the city but of a mercantile alliance created by Hanseatic tradesmen. In all, the alliance included more than 70 northern seaports. The port of Bergen was packed with full riggers. In 1644, some four hundred ships called here from

Scotland alone.

The fjords provide many fine harbours and excellent fishing both in the narrow inlets and in the rich fisheries that lie off the west coast. Today, Norway's shipping and fishing industries rank among the worlds largest. Indeed, fishing is the country's principal industry in most small communities, especially in the Lofoten Islands and the north. Salmon farming with computerised feeding and quality controls has also become big business in the fjords.

So, while one may be forgiven for thinking that the fjords, because of their isolation, cannot really offer much in terms of economic input, the opposite is in fact the case.

Salmon farming ... fishing ... salting and drying cod ... shipping and shipbuilding ... offshore oil ... tanning ... farming and forestry - all these fjord industries have made a significant contribution to the nation's economy. The fjord people are certainly not shy of hard work, which brings me to the story of a most remarkable people - the "real" fjord people, as I call them. The people, in fact, who inspired me to write my lecture and to compile this booklet in the first place.

***

Skageflå Farm, Geirangerfjord.

THE CLIFF TOP FARMERS OF GEIRANGER

There were never more than a couple of hundred of the cliff top farmers, but their lifestyle was one of incredible hardship, extraordinary courage and of a resilience at which the rest of us can only marvel. In many fjords, it is immediately evident that there is not much agricultural land. This is particularly true in the narrower fjords bounded by cliffs that rise almost vertically for a 1,000 feet or more.

Throughout history, people living along Storfjorden - the Great Fjord - left the shoreline settlements and found places for their homes wherever they could. For many of them, that meant farming tiny patches of land on ledges and precipices almost impossibly high above the waters of the fjord.

These isolated farms have been home to farmers and their families for centuries. The mountains and cliffs around Storfjorden *(see map on pages 30-31)* have revealed signs of settlements both from the Stone Age and the Iron Age as well as Viking burial mounds.

Indeed, hardy souls in Geirangerfjord and Sunnylvsfjord eked out a subsistence living from these precipitous farms until the mid 1980s and some of the farms are still worked during the summer months.

These farms are dotted along the innermost part of Storfjorden from Stranda to Valldal and Tafjord, and down to Hellesylt and Geiranger. In those days, tethering the children was common practice. No matter how much they protested, boys and girls up to the age of about ten were tied to a thick rope the moment they left the farmhouse.

It was a simple precaution - and one which, on some farms, was practised even by adults. One need look up from a cruise ship or the Geiranger-Hellesylt ferry to Skageflå and Knivsflå farms to understand why.

At Skageflå, the ascent was so steep that at one point the farmer had to climb an almost vertical ladder to reach the farm. It is difficult to imagine why they chose to live there. In fact, the soil on these mountains is very fertile, so grass and vegetables grow well.

That said, hayfields were often more stone than earth, and instead of scythes the farmers sometimes had to use knives. So, gathering winter hay for the animals was a continuous, backbreaking and dangerous struggle. The wife of one farmer, Anna Matvik, explains:

"They mowed hay up on Korsfjellet mountain, calling it 'The Green'. From there they had a pulley wire which ran right down to the barn. Otherwise, the hay they mowed on three other farms had to go by boat. When they mowed on one farm, it required five different pulley wires even before they could get the hay into the boat.

"Then they had to row to Matvika and by aerial wire up here for drying".

Throughout the summer months, huge bundles of hay whizzed down the mountainsides on a network of aerial cables. Sleek rowing boats with impossibly heavy loads criss-crossed the fjords - only to be hauled up the mountain again to the farm. It was tough, back-breaking lifestyle.

"I had to use six cables to bring the hay down to the shore," says Peter Knivsflå, who farmed a small patch of land next to the Seven Sisters waterfall.

"My brother Martin was about to send down a hay bundle when the wire broke, tossing the lad off the cliff. He fell 30 metres before landing on his feet. His footprints were visible for many years afterwards. He was knocked unconscious and transported to Bergen by fjord steamer. He woke up eight days after and recovered fully and became a great mountaineer."

The path up to Skageflå farm, Geirangerfjord.

The farmers rowed from one side of the fjord to the other, cutting grass from the highest parts of the mountains right down to the water's edge. They climbed after every little grass straw they could find and then rowed back to the other side, and climbed back up to the homestead with massive loads of hay on their backs.

Nor was this a job just for the men. Today, it is almost impossible to imagine living like that especially as before the cable system had to be carried up to the homesteads from the shoreline on people's backs. If there was an iron stove at a farm, that stove would have been hauled up to it.

This was bad enough but in those days there were no special mountaineering boots or trainers with reinforced rubber soles with which to grip the precarious rock paths. All the cliff top farmers had were old-fashioned hobnailed boots.

Nor, in those early days had the farmers hewn any proper paths from the rock. There were no convenient railings to hang onto then, as there are on some of them today. Indeed, it was so dangerous that several farmers - and their womenfolk and children - fell off the cliff top ledges, usually to their deaths. And in winter, of course, it was infinitely worse, but more on that later.

Most of the farmers also had a second farm, known as a "seter". This would normally be situated high above and behind the main farm. Here, the farmers

would keep their animals, notably sheep, goats, and some cattle, which could then graze on the rich grasslands near the summit of the mountains. Sheep and goats were not too much of a problem but pigs were another matter.

One farmer who decided he wanted pigs bought some piglets, took them up to the farm in a sack full of apples and then released them to grow to their full size on the farmstead. Another farmer desperately wanted to have a horse on his smallholding and for years tried to figure out a way of getting one up to his farm.

The only way, of course, was to carry it up. So he bought a new born foal, slung it over his shoulders and lugged it up to the farm where it lived out the rest of its life.

It was, of course, phenomenally hard work and each member of the family was expected to pull their weight. Children learned about toil and hardship at a very early age. At the end of a long day, they rarely complained about going to bed!

The fjord people climbed the cliff face as we would go to the shops or the office, some to fell birch and pine trees. This was an important part of their work, the tree trunks being used for new farm buildings. Apart from the main farmhouse, they needed a cowshed, a barn and a storehouse, a boathouse and often a furnace and a mill, too.

If a farmer had trees on his land, he could count himself lucky. Some had to fell trees else-where, then row the trunks across the fjord, saw the planks at the landing stage and then carry them on weary shoulders up to the homestead. It was a gruelling lifestyle and it was fraught with danger.

Then there were the smaller farms, the seter, which also required their own living quarters, cowshed and barn. The farmer had to build them all himself. Peter Knivsflå recalls:

"Dad sawed every board for them right here on the spot. He used a big handsaw. He laid one log on top and one under while sawing and he sawed every single board in this house with his own two hands".

Theirs was a simple existence with few creature comforts. There was no electricity ... no gas ... and water had to be carried from the nearest stream. They made their own butter and cheese. At one farm, the heavy cheese pan was carried to the farm on the back of a woman guest. But cattle, goats, home-grown vegetables and fish from the fjord ensured they did not go hungry.

By the age of ten, boys and girls were responsible for milking the goats, churning butter and making cheese - even rescuing goats that either fell or became stranded on the cliff face. This was a regular occurrence.

"They would jump down onto the ledges and could not get back up," one farmer explained. "So we lowered the smallest, lightest child down on the end of a rope. The child would cling to the cliff face and tie the goat to the rope. We hoisted it up and then lowered the rope again and the boy was recovered".

"People find it difficult to understand that we left the child on the cliff face, but it was no problem, really. I did it almost every day when I was eight or nine years old, but I was not scared because I trusted my father on the other end of the rope."

Sometimes, the child would simply frighten the goat off the cliff, so that it fell into the water where it could be retrieved by the farmer in a rowing boat. The fjords are almost as full of legends as they are of water. Children were barely out of their cots before they learned the gravity of life. One farm, near Geiranger, was home to six children but the house itself was so small that two of the boys had to sleep in the barn.

The boys were just eight and ten years old when their mother died and her coffin was placed in the barn where they slept. That evening, the boys stood there looking at their mother's body and folded their hands quietly in prayer.

Then, they undressed themselves and climbed into bed at the side of the coffin. It is almost unthinkable today!

Birth, illness and death, in fact, created huge problems for the Fjord People. The fear of becoming ill without being able to get help was ever present and an illness had to be extremely serious before the doctor was called, especially in winter, when the paths were all but impassable.

Moreover, the farmers usually did not have the money to pay, so pain and suffering were also a fact of everyday life.

One woman, who bore no less than eleven children went to the doctor for the first time in her life - at the age of seventy! Another woman was even older doubtless known sickness and pain many times in her life before that.

Nor were there many doctors available. Those who did attend the cliff top farmers needed not only medical skills, but courage, stamina and mountaineering skills as well. One doctor, recalling his days of visiting mountain farms, wrote

somewhat ironically that "through my work I sometimes had the opportunity to drown and sometimes the opportunity to fall to my death".

In winter, a doctor might have to travel as far as possible by boat, then gingerly test the ice and ski across the ice to the landing stage, before climbing the steep mountainside . The danger of being engulfed by an avalanche would never have been far from his mind as he struggled for perhaps five or six miles to reach his patient.

Nor was there any guarantee that he could treat the illness when he got there. One doctor was unable to treat a woman's eye and told her she would have to see a specialist in Bergen.

But Bergen was 250 miles away and the woman and her husband did not have enough money for the journey. So they tied a rope round their ox and set off to walk over the mountains.

When they eventually reached Bergen, they sold the ox and with the money paid for the doctor and for tickets back home on the ferry - a round-trip which took them four weeks.

Still, provided the farmers and their families did not fall off the cliff face, they lived such a healthy lifestyle that they could also expect to have a long life. Most of the farmers and their wives lived to be well over seventy. Many lasted into their nineties - and one woman, Laura Gausdal, celebrated her 106th birthday in 1996. You can see her grave in Geiranger churchyard.

These women were exceptionally tough! One woman remembers how, as a child, she slept in a trough in the kitchen and how, in winter, she would be covered with a dusting of snow when she woke up in the morning.

Her grandmother, Torina Blomberg - who lived to be 100 - was legendary. She had ten children. One day she decided that it was time to have them christened. So she carried all ten children, one by one, down the long and extremely dangerous path to the edge of the fjord.

Once there, she tethered them individually to a tree to keep them out of mischief while she climbed back up to the farm to fetch the next child.

Torina Blomberg with one of her ten children.

Blomberg Farm, where she lived, is 450 metres or 1,350 feet almost sheer above the waterline. That is roughly one-third the height of Mount Snowdon in Wales.

Next, when she had assembled all ten children by the water's edge, she rowed them the seven miles to Geiranger for the christening ceremony. When it was over, she rowed them back to the farm and carried each child - again one by one - up the forty-eight bends to the farm. One feels exhausted just thinking about it – and yet even that epic journey was not the most arduous daring or dangerous journey to be

undertaken in the fjords. That honour has to go to the midwives - and one midwife in particular.

When Jensine Grønningseter found the fjord impassable, she skied 20 miles through the mountains to reach a woman in labour - a journey that took an entire day. Another, elderly midwife, was faced with an exhausting and dangerous climb to a farm above Geiranger. Father and son met her at the shoreline, then guided her up the almost vertical incline - the eldest boy pulling her up with a rope, the young father pushing her up from behind.

"After a while they asked if they were rushing her," Peter Knivsflå relates. "She was a right sprightly lady and said 'No, on you go, lads'. At Bringestølen, they put on skis and just made it in time to receive a baby boy. He is still alive."

The greatest feat of them all, however, was undertaken in the depth of winter by Kristianne Hallsteinsdottir - by no means a spring chicken. Per Rønneberg, another farmer takes up the story.

"During Christmas, a child was born at Knivsflå. They summoned a 75-year-old woman from Gomsdalen.

Kristina Hallsteinsdottir

"To get there as quickly as possible, she travelled along the steep mountainside. She also had to cross what is known as the Deep Crevasse, dropping steeply into the fjord from both veering, perpendicular faces.

"Even for young people in the middle of summer, it is a difficult trek. It is inconceivable how an old woman managed it in mid-winter! She arrived safely, although somewhat late. On entering the farm, she heard a baby boy crying."

Tore Knivsflå , who told the story, said: "I was that boy."

The route taken by Kristianne Halsteinsdotter from Gomsdal to Knifsflå, next to the Seven Sisters waterfall, Geirangerfjord.

An old lady of 75 balancing on small, icy ledges, traversing precipices clogged with snow, fully aware that she faced certain death if she slipped – it seems unbelievable! What phenomenal courage!

When the farmers and their wives grew old, they rarely wanted to leave their homes. They were, after all, used to fending for themselves and they would hang on for as long as they possibly could.

There is a story about one old man who had not been too well and decided, when Autumn came, that he would not last through the coming winter. So he moved down to a cottage by the fjord, where he said wanted to die in order to save his family the hardship of bringing his coffin down in the depths of winter. But when Spring came, the man was not only still alive; he felt much better. So he climbed back up the mountain to spend his last summer on his beloved farm.

Death, though, brought enormous problems. Getting the deceased to the grave, even in summer, was extremely difficult. In winter, it was a nightmare. That a mountain farmer and his family should be buried in consecrated ground was never questioned.

The only issue was when because some of the tracks were so steep and narrow that there was not enough room for two men to walk side by side on them. So coffins often had to be lowered down, dangling, on the end of a rope.

To be a burden to others was the worst fate the Fjord People could imagine. When they thought that death was near, they would normally move down to the water's edge or into the nearest village quietly to prepare for their death. But one farmer became aware of his frailty too late.

When he sensed that the end was near, the snow had already arrived, and lay deep on the mountainside. He knew, of course, of the terrible problems his death would cause for his sons . He told them that if he died, they should place his coffin beneath an overhanging rock and cover it with snow. When he passed away shortly afterwards, they did just that and not until Spring came were they able to dig him out again and finally put him to rest in Geiranger churchyard.

Avalanches were a constant danger and claimed many lives. Some farmers survived by the skin of their teeth. One old man was swept out of bed to find himself halfway down the mountain in his nightshirt. His entire house had been swept away, as had three other farms. But the farmers simply started building again and carried on as if nothing had happened. Such was their lifestyle that they had no other choice.

Two farms at the top of the cliff towering over the Geiranger jetty *(see picture below)* had to be abandoned after avalanches swept 13 people to their deaths. The survivor of another avalanche describes what it was like.

Avalanche in Geirangerfjord and, below, Vesterås Farm seen from above as opposed to from the water's edge (see page 6)

"The entire house began trembling and shaking. I tried to get as close to the buttress as possible. The house was crowded with folks, both young and old. The avalanche broke a few joists in the barn roof, otherwise nothing.

"Obviously, it was dangerous to be outside the house, but we needed a man to stand watch in order to see exactly when the avalanche started far above. As the avalanche approached, he would shout so everyone remained indoors. Then the scout would duck for cover as fast as possible."

Thin ice on the fjord was similarly hazardous.

"The entire house began trembling and shaking"

"The men would drag a boat across the ice and where the men and a boat could go, we kids could safely follow. If the men went through the ice, they just climbed out, hauled the boat back onto the ice and continued. It happened often, but we always managed."

In summer, the problem was rockslides. The most tragic of these was in April 1934, when an enormous mountain overhang crashed into the fjord. The resulting flood wave was said to be sixty metres or 180 feet at its highest. It almost completely wiped out two villages. When it had receded, forty people had lost their lives. Later, it was calculated that a buttress containing three million cubic meters of rock had fallen into the fjord.

One woman - who was 11 years old at the time - actually

remembers seeing the wave. She said it swept away everything in its path - people, houses and trees - and that when it hit the electricity transformer, the noise, flames and the colours were incredible. Years later, she visited the 1992 Winter Olympics at Lillehammer in Norway. She described the spectacular opening firework ceremony - as being "quite bleak" compared with what she had seen that evening.

Incidentally, another buttress of rock not far from the mouth of Geirangerfjord, is being monitored. Vertical cracks suggest it, too, will fall into the fjord. *(see photograph page 43)*. With an estimated 21 million cubic metres of rock expected to tumble into the fjord, it will have disastrous consequences.

Researchers have calculated that the wave it creates will take just eight minutes to reach the little town of Hellesylt. The town's fate can only be imagined. Not surprisingly, local authorities have put into place a sophisticated alarm system and have drawn up contingency plans for a mass evacuation. In 2006, the buttress was monitored as having moved considerably, although experts expect it will be several more So the Fjord People paid – and still do pay - heavily for their peaceful coexistence with Nature. It was not just the tracks, the precipices and the avalanches that were so dangerous. The fjord itself was no less so.

Sudden, downward gusts of wind can whip the water into the equivalent of a Force 5 sea. Anybody in a rowing boat had more than enough to cope with. And several boats went down with their occupants. For many children, rowing boats were the only means of getting to school at the nearest village, a journey that could take several hours. That, of course, made it difficult for them to return home in the evenings so they would stay with the villagers for two or three weeks at a time.

On one trip, a boat packed with schoolchildren was nearly wrecked when a wave washed into the boat, half filling it with water. Fortunately, a quick thinking farmer immediately emptied the milk churn and used it as a bailer and was thus able to save them.

After that, the children went to another school where they could stay with relatives, but it meant that they were only able to go home on festive occasions and during the summer holidays.

So it was a lonely life, as well. One farmer at Knivsflå next to the Seven Sisters waterfall in Geirangerfjord was so lonely that he invited his brother-in-law to move in and take over half the farm.

They had to build a new farmhouse, barn and loft, but from that day on there were two farms at Knivsflå. Meanwhile, at Skrednakken farm nearby, a young housewife had a particularly lonely existence. Anna Matvik explains.

"While her husband was by the shore fixing up some timber she got so lonely she wanted to join him. She was expecting her first child in three week's time, so she was heavy.

And the snow was deep and the hillside very steep. Nevertheless she felt relieved by the few words she had If Elida Tafjord wanted company, she had to row across the fjord from Vikasetra to the small town of Sylte *(see map pp.30-31)* and many was the time after an exhausting day that she would dance until sunrise and then row home again, climb back up to the farm and immediately start a new day's work.

Elida Tafjord

During the final winter of World War Two, Elida hid six escaped Russian prisoners-of-war in her family's summer farm at the top of the mountain. Not even her own mother knew that each night she climbed through the snow to take them food. The last climb was on the night of May the 8th, 1946.

"I put on knee breeches and boots and ran all the way to the she says. "I told them they could come down because finally the war was over.

"They were jubilant. They followed me down and I shoved out the boat, but none of them could row. So I rowed alone and told them all to sit down. Elida, of course, saved their lives and several of the Russians have returned to visit her since.

A deep faith and the local church helped the Fjord People cope with the dangers, the loneliness and the hardship, and there are many stories of rock- slides and avalanches that stopped abruptly behind a house filled with God-fearing people.

Today, it is difficult to grasp how the first farmers could even reach these mountain farms. Nor should we forget that at times, the paths up to the farms were so steep they had to climb up wooden ladders in order to surmount a rock overhang - and often did so bearing huge bales of hay on their backs.

Just occasionally, though, there was a distinct advantage to the loneliness and inaccessibility of the cliff top farms. At Skageflå Farm in Geirangerfjord, the farmer is said to have kept a sharp eye out for visiting tax authorities. When they arrived, he would simply haul up the ladder - and the tax men had no alternative but to return whence they came.

***

THE END OF AN ERA

You may recall that I mentioned the farmer who was so lonely that he asked his brother-in-law to take over half his farm above Geiranger. That farm is abandoned now. The local government decided that the danger of an overhang falling and crushing the farm, and its occupants was too great.

Today, a hundred years later, the overhang is still there - as indeed is the farm, now fully renovated. However, more than a hundred farms along the steep mountainsides have been abandoned. Most of the farmers and their families left just after the Second World War as the industrial society developed and jobs and money attracted the youngsters to the towns. It's a familiar story.

The prime reason for abandoning the farms was a government regulation which dictated that all children of school age must attend school every day. Consequently, if life on the farms was to continue at all, it would have to be without children. For the cliff top farmers that would have been a completely meaningless existence.

The only answer was to move. Gradually, the farmers gradually left their birthplaces and childhood homes, their farms and their life's work. It was a bitter

disappointment. The last family came down just before Christmas in 1981 to a world which, confusingly to them , seemed to be dependant entirely on clocks, machines, stress and noise, and on consumerism and egotism.

Of all the hardships they had faced this was probably the most difficult of them all, especially as they knew that the old farms would gradually crumble and fall into a state of disrepair, as indeed they did.

The good news is that in recent years, the Fjord People have attracted growing interest. It is as if we want their farms to stand as permanent monuments to their strength, their courage and their moral fortitude.; a reminder, if you like, of how perhaps we would like to be ourselves - living away from the hustle and bustle of modern life with all its stresses and strains and instead living a hard but rewarding life in some of the most beautiful surroundings on earth.

In 1975, a group of interested people founded a Society of Friends with members from all parts of the world. It began with just eight members. Today, there are well over 1,000.

Each summer, they come to the Great Fjord and set about restoring the different buildings. The old owners are returning, too, to protect their farms from the corrosive elements of Nature and, in a few cases, even to farm them again during the summer months.

If original fire has been extinguished, the Friends have rekindled a new flame representing the spirit of the Fjord People. Long may it burn!

***

SAIL-AWAY GUIDE

From

Geiranger to Hellesylt & Sunnylvsfjord

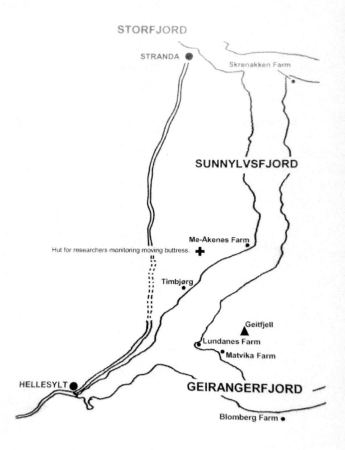

NORRDALSFJORD   SYLTE

• Vikasetra

NORRDAL

TAFJORD

During the second world war, Elida Tafjord secretly fed six Russian prisoners of war hidden at Vikasetra. Each evening, without fail, she would climb up with food supplies and thus saved the Russians lives.

Seven Sisters • Knivsflå Farm

GOMSDAL

Horvadraget   Skageflå   • Bringa   Eagle's Highway

The Pulpit
Homlong   Vesterås Farm

GEIRANGER

GEIRANGER VILLAGE

Geiranger has a resident population of only 270 souls. The first tourists came here in 1869 – and their number has increased year on year ever since. Now, between 160 and 170 cruise ships visit the fjord between early May and late September each year, disgorging about 160,000 passengers.

Another 25,000-50,000 people arrive here from central Europe and elsewhere, which means that this tiny village welcomes nearly quarter of a million people each year. In winter, of course, it is as quiet as the grave.

Geiranger Church and its graveyard overlooking the fjord tell a remarkable history of fortitude and hardship.

Look back from your ship to the top of the rock face immediately above Geiranger and you may be able to see a flagpole and some wooden buildings right on the edge of the cliff. These were part of two farms called Vesterås and Holeback.

On 22nd February 1907, an avalanche swept down from the 4,500 feet,or 1500 metres high mountain, Laushorn, behind them, killing three people. Worse, the following morning, a second avalanche all but destroyed the farms and killed another ten people. It was just one of many black days experienced in this fjord.

Rock falls and avalanches were commonplace - and a constant threat: the price the farmers had to pay for the privilege of living in such beautiful surroundings.

Vesterås and Holeback farms, Geirangerfjord

HOMLONG

As the ship leaves Geiranger, look to your left, off the port bow towards the holiday chalets at the water's edge. This once was Homlong farm. Directly above it, you can the upper farm buildings in the trees at the top of the rocks. About ten feet or three metres behind them is a 750 foot (250 metre) – sheer drop.

Homlong farm was home to a God-fearing family who were extremely devout. On one occasion, the family huddled in the main building as a huge avalanche roared down the mountainside.

They were convinced they would die and prayed intensely. As they did so, the avalanche careered towards them - but stopped miraculously just a few feet away from the farm buildings.

There were many farmers in Geiranger and along the fjord who were convinced that this was a

miracle down to the Lord's benevolence.

Years later, however, another avalanche wiped out several buildings of the lower farm – which is now the holiday centre that you can see.

Homlong Farm

750ft (250m)

EAGLE'S HIGHWAY

On the opposite bank, to starboard, is a road known as the Eagle's Highway - a fearsome set of hairpin bends that seem tame enough from the fjord but which in places are quite terrifying – and offer spectacular views of the fjord. The road has a 1 in 12 gradient and to make it even more exciting, it is a single lane highway for most of the way. Considered a marvel of Norwegian engineering upon its completion in 1952, the highway climbs to 620 metres - just over 2,000 feet - and after a two-hour drive across the mountains, it takes you down the even more terrifying Troll's Highway down to the towns of Eidsvall and Åndalsnes.

The hotel at the base of the Eagle's Highway, incidentally, is one of four major hotels in Geiranger.

EAGLE'S HIGHWAY

← BRINGA

THE PULPIT

To the left, off the port side, you can see a large buttress of rock jutting out from the cliff. This is known as Prekkestolen - the Priest's Chair - or more commonly "The Pulpit".

BRINGA

The farmer's wife who lived in the small house just above the water's edge just to the left of the Eagle's Highway (on the right or starboard side of the ship leaving Geiranger) was extremely devout. This farm had especially fertile soil and because it was sheltered and therefore tended to be frost-free throughout the winter, hops grew there particularly well. The lady of house, who name was Ragnhild, was known far and wide for brewing fantastic beer. But just to be safe, she chanted both pagan and Christian prayers to make absolutely sure of retaining the superiority of her brew.

GOMSDALEN

To the left of Bringa and the Eagle's Highway, you will see a waterfall, at the top of which is a fertile valley called Gomsdal. In 1892, this was the starting point for Kristianne Halsteinsdottir, the 75-year-old midwife who traversed in the thick of winter the almost vertical cliffs and icy Paths to Knivsflå Farm immediately to the right of the Seven Sisters waterfall. *(See pp 17-18)*.

It was an incredible feat. Even today, mountaineers with all their equipment, find it impossible to believe that an old woman could achieve such a thing. Not surprisingly perhaps, she arrived too late and heard the sound of baby boy crying. The man who told that story, Tore Knivsflå, said:

"That baby was me". He died in 1986 aged 94, and is buried in Geiranger churchyard.

People communicated with each other in an emergency like that by lighting candles in their windows at night or by sending smoke signals by day. The number of candles, or puffs of smoke determined the kind of emergency. Three candles, for example, would be shown if a doctor was needed.

KNIVSFLÅ

Knivsflå was so isolated that the boy's father suffered terribly from loneliness, so he asked his brother-in-law to build a second farm on the site. From that day on, local council feared that a huge rock overhang would fall down and crush the houses.

The owners moved their home to Geiranger but continued to use the land up at Knivsflå until the 1980s. The overhanging rock, incidentally, is still there and the farm, now completely renovated, is still farmed during the summer months.

Knivsflå Farm, Geirangerfjord

Knivsflå Farm

Seven Sisters Waterfall

SKAGEFLÅ FARM

The most dramatic off all the cliff top farms, Skageflå , is best seen from the Seven Sisters waterfall, looking backwards and to the right of the fjord (i.e. on the port side of the ship). Perched 850 feet, or 300 metres, on a tiny shelf of fertile land. This was the farm from which the youngest or lightest child was lowered down the precipitous cliff face clinging to a rope to save stranded goats.

Children of eight to ten years old, being the lightest in the family, would regularly be lowered - perhaps several times a week - down the cliff face onto a small ledge, from which they would throw stones to frighten the goat and force it to jump into the water.

The farmer would haul it into his rowing boat. Sometimes, the child would be lowered down and left on the ledge whilst the goat wasNhauled up. The farmer above would then lower the rope so that the child could be pulled back up again.

In the old days, you could only reach Skageflå Farm from the water's edge and the route up to it was tortuous *(see diagram above)* with the final few metres accessible only up a vertical wooden ladder.It seems almost unbelievable that men and women climbed that path and that ladder wearing only hobnailed boots, with no handrails and perhaps carrying huge bales of hay on their backs. On occasion, though, the vertical ladder could be quite convenient, not least when the taxman arrived. Then, the farmer simply pulled up the ladder.

The taxman, of course, threatened police and prosecution but the farmer just smiled and walked away, thus delaying payment of his taxes for at least another year!

The route up to Skageflå Farm from the fjord. There was alsoa back way up from Homlong and over The Pulpit to the farm. The 'taxman's ladder was just beneath the "P" of 'Pulpit' in the diagram.

The youngest child would be lowered on a rope to rescue a goat, usually by frightening it off a ledge so that it fell into the water, where an older member of the family would haul it into a rowing boat.

SEVEN SISTERS WATERFALL

The Seven Sisters waterfall is probably the most famous in all Norway. The falls are 1,345 feet or 410 metres high. However, in summer, when the family can increase to as many as a dozen or more 'sisters'. They may even merge so that it becomes difficult to count them. At other times, especially in late summer, the falls may be reduced to a mere trickle and there may be as few as four falls.

Western Norway, incidentally, consists of a mountainous mass of ancient Cambrian granite, interspersed with layers of sedimentary rocks like limestone and beds of slate, slashed through by countless years of escaping ice.

BRIDE'S VEIL

The waterfalls along Geiranger are fed, of course, by melting snows . On average they are about 750 feet or 250 metres high, although some are much higher than that. Over the years, almost all the waterfalls have been named and there are many stories and legends about each of them.

Most of these tales, of course, have been invented and perpetuated by people in the tourist industry. A good example is the Seven Sister's waterfall. One of the falls is known as the "Bridal Veil" because of the spray that often blows from it.

THE SUITOR

On the opposite side of the fjord, on the left or port side of the ship, is another waterfall. This is called "The Suitor". Legend has it that ever since the fjord was created by the ice grinding its way down to the sea 60 or so miles away, the Suitor has pined for his bride-to-be on the opposite bank, unable even to touch her or kiss her hand. The Suitor's only hope of wedding his love is if

the spray that forms the Bride's Veil should mingle with the spray from the Suitor's cloak. In that event, the waters of the fjord will drain away into the sea and the couple finally will be able to marry. Believe that, you'll believe anything!

HORVADRAGET & MEGAARDSPLASSEN

These two farms were just to the left of the Seven Sisters waterfall. There is only one small cabin there now. Megaardsplassen is a little higher up and to the left of Horvadraget. Marks of a huge rock fall can be seen between Horvadraget and Seven Sisters.

BLOMBERG FARM

As the ship passes the Seven Sisters and Hovadraget farm, look ahead and to the left of the ship. This is Blomberg Farm, which means "Flower Mountain". It has one of the most beautiful views of the Geirangerfjord. The farm lies 1,350 feet or about 450 metres above the fjord.

The beginning of the path up to it is just to the left of the waterfall. The path climbs through the forest and is extremely steep with no fewer than 48 hairpin bends to climb. At the top, the path is almost vertical. This was the home of a woman who lived to be 100 years old. She had ten children

and one day she decided that she would have them all christened.

Amazingly, she carried all ten children down the long and extremely dangerous switchback path, one by one, to the water's edge. Once there, she would tether each child to an tree and then climb the path once more to collect the next child.

Once she had assembled all ten children, she rowed them the seven miles back to Geiranger village for the christening ceremony. The christening ceremony over, she then repeated the process in reverse.

The small house to the right of the waterfall , incidentally, is another farm called "Syltevika". One of the girls who lived at Blomberg tells how she slept in a trough in the kitchen and in winter woke up covered with snow. (*See photo next page)*

Blommerg farm is quite difficult to see – you need to look for the horizontal ridge and, with binoculars, you should then just be able to see the farm building.

MATVIKA AND LUNDANES

As the ship approaches the mouth of Geirangerfjord, there is a small farm on the starboard (right) side of the ship quite close to the water's edge. This is known as Matvika - which means "Food Cove". It was said the farmer there grew the best tomatoes in the fjord. The farm was also renowned for its apples, peaches and apricots. Most of these farms had an upper farm called a 'seter'. If you let your eye travel up the deep gully that goes all the way from Matvika up to the snowline - that is where the seter was! *(See photograph and diagram)*

Matvika Farm, Geirangerfjord.

After a hard day's work, a young woman who yearned for company of her own age would often row from Matvika across to village of Hellesylt, on the port (left) side at the end of Sunnylvsfjord. She would then row back in the early hours of the morning, catch a couple of hour's sleep and begin another day's work.

Lundanes farm, also on the water's edge, which you will see on your right as we come out of Geirangerfjord and turn right into Sunnylvsfjord, also had a seter high up on the mountain. *(See diagram on page 39)*.

The farmers kept several dairy cows, a horse and goats up there. Indeed, the mountain behind them is called Geitfjell or Goat Mountain. One of the farmers told how it took him an hour to climb up there and, after a day's work, 45 minutes to come down again. He would then row across to Hellesylt which took another hour, read the lesson or say some prayers in the church before rowing home again for his evening meal.

Devout people, indeed!

Lundanes ('nes' meaning 'nose' or small headland) has a natural landing place and it is thought that this is the oldest farm in the convoluted fjord system that comprises Storfjord, or "The Great Fjord".

The farmer who lived here found many examples of flint, suggesting that it was once a site where weapons were made. He also found a bronze ring and several round stones that almost certainly were part of a Viking farm.

In Viking times, the trees grew right down to the shoreline - which was good for house and boat building – but which also meant that there was very little agricultural land, which was one of the principal reasons why the Vikings went on raiding missions and settled abroad.

Only the eldest son could inherit a farm and thus be wealthy enough to pay the mandatory house bond to the bride's father. 'House bond', incidentally, is the origin of the word 'husband'.

If younger sons, who could not inherit, wished to marry, they had to seek their fortune abroad , which was bad news for the monasteries of Scotland, England, Ireland and France.

Contrary to popular opinion, however, the Vikings never sought to have an empire . They were essentially farmers and all they wanted to do was to settle down with a family on their own farm.

In every instance, once they had conquered a people, they then integrated into their society and lived peacefully with them thereafter.

HELLYSYLT, SUNNYLYVSFJORD AND TAFJORD

As the ship emerges from Geirangerfjord, you will see the village of Hellesylt at the southern end of the Sunnylvsfjord to your left.

Hellesylt Village

Your ship will turn quite quickly to starboard (right) and head northeast and north along Sunnylvsfjord. After a few minutes, you will see quite clearly off the port side, the road and tunnels leading to Stranda and some wooden buildings with steeply angled corrugated iron roofs.

These comprise a farm called Me-Åkenes.

The farmer and his family deliberately placed the buildings as close to the mountainside as they could - and whenever it was thought there was a danger of a rock slide or an avalanche they would post a lookout who would shout a warning - and then dash inside at the last minute.

Several avalanches have hit the building's steeply angled roof, but none have caused any serious damage. Immediately above the farm, at the top of the wide gully and slightly to the right of it, there is a small grey hut in which scientists are measuring the movement of a truly massive buttress of rock.

This buttress contains an estimated twenty-one million cubic metres of rock and it is expected at some stage to fall into the fjord. If it does so, it will create a huge wave which it is calculated would take only eight minutes to reach the village of Hellesylt, now directly behind the ship.

Previous experience of such rock falls has been disastrous. In April, 1934, a buttress containing some three million cubic metres of rock fell into the fjord near Taffjord, causing a mini-tsunami 64 metres or nearly 200 feet high.

That happened in the arm of the fjord which will shortly strike off to the right. The damage resulting from a wave caused by a rock fall seven times bigger can only be imagined. Such events were - and still are - fairly common along Storfjorden.

Hut in which researchers are monitoring the movement of the 21 million cubic metre buttress above. If it falls into the fjord, the resultant 'tsunami' is expected to engulf Hellesylt in eight minutes.

Me-Åkenes Farm

In 1905, 61 people were killed when another rockslide crashed into the fjord - again close to Tafjord.

In a similar accident in 1936, another buttress containing an estimated one million cubic metres of rock collapsed and created an even bigger wave. This was estimated to have been 75 metres or 225 feet high. It devastated two villages and killed 74 people.

At this stage, it is perhaps worth reflecting that two million years ago, the valleys and fjords that we see today did not exist, but were instead covered with ice two thousand feet thick. The remnants of it still exist in the form of Jostedalsbreen, the largest icecap in northern Europe. It lies just over the mountains behind Hellesylt and beyond the southerly bank of Geirangerfjord.

Whenever I give a talk on cruise ships about Geiranger and Sunnylvsfjord, I always tell my audience that once they have learned more about the lifestyle of cliff top farmers and their families, they will never forget them.

I sincerely hope this modest booklet similarly will serve as a reminder of these extraordinary and inspiring people.

Sam Hall

Printed in Great Britain
by Amazon